Peter Paul Rubens

Detail from Plate XI-XII.

Funk & Wagnalls, Inc., New York

MICHAEL JAFFE

FELLOW OF KING'S COLLEGE, CAMBRIDGE; UNIVERSITY LECTURER IN THE HISTORY OF ART

Peter Paul Rubens 1577-1640

The sixth child of Jan Rubens and Maria Pypelinckx was born at Siegen (Germany) on June 28, 1577, and named next day for Saints Peter and Paul, whose feast it then was. His father, though born Catholic, had had, because of Calvinist leanings, to leave the Spanish Netherlands. Settling first in Cologne, he had all but forfeited his life through the discovery of his liaison with Princess Anna of Saxony, whom he had served officially as a diplomatic advisor.

When Jan died in 1587, his widow felt free to return to Antwerp, where both her family and that of her errant husband had been prosperously settled. Education, begun for Peter Paul and his elder brother Philip with their learned father, developed at Verdonck's Latin School. There Peter Paul befriended a future patron, Balthasar Moretus, heir to the Plantin Press. The call to provide her daughter's dowry forced Maria Rubens to send Peter Paul, aged fourteen, to make his own living as a page in a noble household. Soon tiring of courtly service, he persuaded his mother to have him trained as a painter: first with her kinsman Verhaeght; then with Van Noort; and finally, for almost four years, with the most distinguished of the Antwerp Romanists, Otto van Veen.

On May 9, 1600, two years after he had been accepted as a master, Peter Paul left for Italy 'in order to study at close quarters the works of the ancient and modern masters and to improve himself in painting by their example'. He went first to Venice, where he obtained a fortunate introduction to Vincenzo I Gonzaga, who employed him at Mantua.

By 1602, Peter Paul had visited every artistic centre of note in Italy: including Florence in October, 1600, for the marriage by proxy of the Duchess of Mantua's sister, Marie de'Medici; and Rome for the winter of 1601-02. In the metropolis he obtained his first public commission through his fellow countryman, Jean Richardot: three altarpieces for the chapel of St. Helena, in Santa Croce in Gerusalemme. In 1603 he was entrusted with his first diplomatic mission, to take gifts to Philip III and his court. In Madrid and at the Escorial he had his first sight of the Hapsburg collections, including more than seventy works by Titian; and at Valladolid he painted for the Duke of

Lerma a superb equestrian portrait, besides a Democritus and Heraclitus to replace copies of Italian masterpieces irreparably damaged on the journey. He returned via Genoa to recover expenses from Vincenzo's banker, Nicolo Pallavacini, at whose cost he was to paint for S. Ambrogio there The Circumcision (1605), and The Miracle of St. Francis Xavier (1619). For the principal chapel of the Jesuit church in Mantua he painted three huge canvases (1604-05). Through another member of the Genoese banking patriciate, Monsignor Jacopo Serra, he gained the most coveted commission in the Rome of 1606, the high altarpiece for the Oratorian Chiesa Nuova; and thereby in 1608 a commission for the Oratorians at Fermo. His work for the Roman Oratory was barely finished when he had to ride post-haste to Antwerp, recalled by Philip's news that their mother was dying.

Peter Paul reached home too late to see her alive. His first altarpiece for the Chiesa Nuova, painted on canvas, for which he himself had proposed a replacement on slates (because of adverse lighting), became her funeral monument. Within a few months of his return to Flanders he was 'bound with golden fetters' to the Hapsburg Regents, the Infanta Isabella and the Archduke Albert. In October, 1609, he married Isabella, daughter of Jan Brandt, a lawyer and humanist. He established himself as the leading painter of his country by a trilogy of monumental works: The elevation of the Cross (1609-10), for St. Walpurga's, Antwerp; The Deposition (1611-14), for Antwerp Cathedral; and The Conversion of St. Bavon (National Gallery, London). In January, 1611, he bought the land in Antwerp on which to construct his famous house and garden. By May that year his studio was over-full; more than a hundred would-be pupils had to be turned away.

For the church of the Antwerp Jesuits, he acted both as adviser on design and master-decorator in sculpture and painting (contracts of 1614 and 1620). 1621 marked a turning point in his career: on April 9, the Twelve Years' Truce ended, and on July 13, the Archduke Albert died, leaving the painter for the next twelve years intensely busy as trusted adviser in diplomacy to the widowed

Infanta; moreover, in June his chief engraver, Lucas Vorsterman, by whose skill Rubens' international reputation was increasing, had a serious break-down. Nevertheless, major contracts came from abroad as well as from Flanders: twelve models for a tapestry on The Life of Constantine (1621, for Louis XIII); two vast cycles of political allegories to decorate galleries in the new Palais de Luxembourg, of which the first was delivered in 1625 (for Marie de'Medici); tapestry designs on The Triumph of the Eucharist for the convent of the Descalzas Reales, Madrid (1626-28, for the Infanta Isabella); and two related commissions for London ceilings, The Triumph of the Duke of Buckingham (by 1628) for York House, and nine pieces for the Banqueting House in Whitehall (ready 1634, for Charles I).

The death of his wife in 1626 overtaxed the Christian stoicism of Rubens. He was the readier to immerse himself in diplomatic voyages to Spain, France, Holland and England, where at last he achieved his own 'Project for the Cessation of Arms' on behalf of Spain and the Spanish Netherlands. His last years were made happy by freedom to pursue undistracted his 'dolcissima professione', to enjoy and paint landscapes in the neighbourhood of his Château de Steen; and by his family life.

In December, 1630, he wedded Hélèna Fourment, the sixteen-year-old niece of his first wife. Two sons survived from the earlier marriage, and by Hélèna he had three daughters and two more sons. In 1636 he was appointed court painter to the Infanta's successor, the Infante Ferdinand. To solemnise this successful general's Triumphal Entry into impoverished Antwerp two years earlier, he – with every painter in the city working to his direction – had turned the streets into a gigantic theatre. Through the Infante was arranged his last contract (1636) for the Hapsburgs, the furnishing of a hundred and twenty painted mythologies for Philip IV's hunting box near Madrid. In this mammoth task he trusted assistants to an unwonted degree to paint the canvases from his sketches. He was pressed for delivery; and frequently his painting arm was crippled by gout, of which he had first complained in January, 1627. He died on May 30, 1640, when the gout reached his heart.

'Rubens is still Rubens even if he did come a hundred years after the immortals of Italy . . . He adorns his century simply by his own existence, instead of being one of a company of other talents that contribute to its splendour.' — DELACROIX

THE MOST FAMOUS citizen of Antwerp, and her greatest artist was born in an obscure town in Westphalia. He did not see his own country until he was almost ten. Nearly thirty years later his choice of what to paint as an altarpiece for the private chapel of the Archduke Albert in Brussels is revealing, *The Return of the Holy Family from Egypt* (Wadsworth Atheneum, Hartford, Conn.). In composing this subject, hitherto scarcely treated in painting, he studied the head and feet of the Archduke's godson, his own son Albert, for those of the Christ Child. This masterpiece, which he got Vorsterman to engrave after a model drawn for the purpose by Van Dyck, signifies how keenly he knew the meaning and joy of a family's home-coming from exile.

He and Philip, the brother to whom he was closest, were baptised of necessity as Lutherans. In Antwerp they became, as their mother had devotedly remained, regularly observant Catholics. Peter Paul painted altarpieces successively for the Jesuit Churches in Mantua, Genoa, Neuburg, Antwerp and Ghent. In Antwerp he designed a title-page for Father Cornelissen's 'Commentary on the Pentateuch' —the inspiration of Bernini's early altar tabernacle in S. Agostino, and illustrations, as well as a title-page, for Father Aguilon's 'Six Books on Optics'. He was a friend of Father Tiry, the Jesuit Provincial; he frequented the Maison Professe in Antwerp, where he was a member of the Grand Sodality of the Annunciation; and his ideas, culled from the vault of S. Andrea in Mantua, from the courtyard of the Cancellaria in Rome, and from architectural features of S. Maria di Carignano and the palaces in Genoa (plans and elevations of which he published in 1622), were adopted for the spectacular new church of St. Ignace by Father Huyssens, who had not then been to Italy. Surviving drawings show indeed how Rubens was responsible for almost every detail of the enrichment of this extravagantly sumptuous temple; from the pattern of the black and white marble pavement to the embroidery on the cope; from the statuary in the tympanum to the precise form of the chalice. He stood as close as a layman could to this militant company in his generation; much as Bernini, the second genius of the Baroque, would in his. But no more than Bernini's, is Rubens' style when working for the Catholic church to be identified as 'le style jésuite'. He painted altarpieces in Rome for the Oratorians, although meanness and dilatoriness over payment made him curse the dealings of the Roman Fathers. In Antwerp he worked for Augustinians, Recollects, Norbertines and Dominicans. For the Dominican church he painted a *Disputà* and a *Flagellation*; and he was a leading subscriber with his friend Jan Bruegel to purchase a third distinctively Dominican altarpiece, Caravaggio's *Madonna of the Rosary*, which his senior contemporary as a Flemish painter in Mantuan service, Frans Pourbus, had found homeless on the Italian market after the painter's death. Rubens' confessor, Michael Ophovius, was a Dominican. But his funerary chapel, for which he painted the altarpiece with himself in the guise of St. George, is in his own parish church of St. Jacques.

MINDFUL ALWAYS of what Protestantism and exile could mean in the life of a man and his family, Rubens conformed: but in the strength of his nature he was not pinioned. He was devout, and sincere in his devotion. The Christian stoicism, by which he withstood the disappointments and intrigues of a war-torn Europe, however inadequate it was to prevent his giving way to natural grief at the sudden loss of his excellent and beloved Isabella Brandt, had no doubt been fostered in him by his brother Philip. With him he was brought up; with him he corresponded, while he himself was in the first years of his Italian venture and Philip, as a young graduate, was tutoring the Richardot boys; with him he shared a house and servants, and a passion for the surviving relics of antiquity, during the second, extended period of his studies in Rome (1605-08), while Philip prepared himself for civic office or a university chair at home by working as librarian to Cardinal Ascanio Colonna. Philip's intellectual master was Justus Lipsius, who corresponded with Pope Paul V as his admired Seneca was reputed to have done with Nero. Peter Paul, working for the Plantin Press, designed title-pages both for Lipsius' edition of Seneca (1615) and for his complete works (1637). Symbolic of this interest are paintings (c. 1611-14) which he based on a marble head, of the type which in the seventeenth century was believed to portray Seneca, and of which he treasured an example with other antiquities in the domestic Pantheon attached to his house in Antwerp: one with Seneca envisaged in the stark greyness of death (Staatliche Kunsthalle, Karlsruhe); one with Seneca's dying words being recorded by a devoted disciple (Bayerische Staatsgemäldesammlungen, Munich), the philosopher's body being modelled on that of the so-called *Nile Fisherman*, a life-size marble in the Borghese collection which Rubens had drawn from every angle as a young enthusiast in Rome; and one, painted a decade earlier, with the busts of Seneca and Nero (Private Collection, London) relished side by side, full-blooded as men larger than life. But the most humanly expressive of all is where the *Seneca* appears simply as itself in a niche, sightless but penetrating, the presence which broods over *Justus Lipsius and his Pupils* (Plate III). Lipsius had died in 1606, his pupil Philip Rubens five years later. The group commemorates friendship; the living being represented by Jan van den Wouwere, a fellow-pupil with Philip under Lipsius, and the painter himself. Peter Paul stands behind his brother almost as the *Seneca* supports Lipsius: for only three or four years beforehand Philip's 'Electorum Libri II' (Antwerp, 1608) had issued from the Plantin Press, to which work of classical scholarship, Peter Paul had contributed decidedly more than just the drawings for the plates. And the painting of this group may have been occasioned by the more recent publication of 'Woverius'.

IN THE BACKGROUND of *Justus Lipsius and his Pupils* is a view of the ruins of the Palatine, based on sketches made by Rubens in Rome, such as he had used in painting as early as 1606 for the background of the demonstration

1. DEPOSITION
Rijksmuseum, Amsterdam

piece by which he secured the Chiesa Nuova commission, and such as provided motifs also for at least two independent landscapes designed to evoke Rome in the years closely following his return to Antwerp. Indeed active recollections of his crucially formative experience of Italy and Italian art lasted, with supple changes of emphasis, to the end of his career. To Peter Paul, son of Jan Rubens, and pupil of Otto van Veen, who had spent six years south of the Alps, Italy was not only the noblest repository of painting, sculpture and architecture, but the eternal home of all the arts of civilisation. He came to know the Italian cities and countryside as few from the North have ever done; and he saw the masterpieces of the Renaissance almost all in their intended places. Of the six languages of which he acquired a working knowledge, Italian remained his favourite for correspondence; and he wrote it as if Tuscan born. Although after he rode from Rome in 1608 he hankered in vain to return there, or to Genoa where he had also established a reputation, he continued to sign himself Pietro Paolo Rubens. He maintained connections with Genoese families, members of which he had glorified in portraiture in 1606-07, by supplying from Antwerp not only cartoons for tapestry on *The History of Decius Mus*, (about 1617), and shortly afterwards a second altarpiece for their Jesuit church, but also Flemish landscapes from the period of his ownership of the Château de Steen. To the Grand Ducal collection of Tuscany which he saw first in 1600, he despatched in 1638 the great canvas of *The Horrors of War* (Uffizi, Florence). And it was probably Cardinal Francesco Barberini in Rome, earlier persuaded

by Louis XIII to accept the *History of Constantine* series as a diplomatic present, who commissioned directly for his tapestry factory the series on *The History of Achilles*.

Even before Rubens set out for Italy he had studied Italian design through prints. Thus he may have made his elaborate copies in red and black chalks of Michelangelo's *Prophets* and *Sybils* (Fig. 2) before he ever entered the Sistine Chapel to record there with greater freedom, even violence, the impact of what he saw. Through van Veen's tastes he would have been introduced to the serene *Annunciation* etched by Barocci, the formal suggestion for his dramatic reinterpretation of the subject soon after his return from Italy (Plate I). In the head and draperies of his Gabriel, Rubens galvanised the recollection of the corresponding figure in Titian's famous polyptych in Brescia. But the system of rendering flesh by subtle juxtaposition of bluish, rosy and yellowish patches of local colour stems from the Barocci altarpieces which he had more recently seen each day at the Chiesa Nuova. It had been hard to invigorate the style of flesh painting in which Rubens had been trained by van Veen with the look of life. Only from about 1614 did he develop effectively his own vibrant technique in realising warm and cool oscillations of light by glazing pigments onto panels smoothly prepared with gesso, across which charcoal had been striped diagonally so as to vary both luminosity and the optical values of the flesh colour as that was brushed over streaks and interstices. This technique, the envy and despair of painters from Nattier to Renoir, Rubens brought eventually to its nacreous perfection in his *Portrait of Susanne Fourment* (Plate XIII), the elder sister of his second wife, and in *Hélèna Fourment Dandling her Son Frans* (Plate X). But from work even before 1600 we can observe his lifelong predilections for the pulsating effect of red in half-tones and reflections, in skillfully scattered accents as well as in draperies, enhancing the vitality of his figures.

IN VENICE, WHITHER RUBENS was able to return several times during his Mantuan service, certain places seem especially redolent of his passionate interest: the Scuola di S. Marco, and the Scuola di S. Rocco ablaze with the fiery brilliance of Jacopo Tintoretto's late works; the church of S. Sebastiano, luxurious with the decorations of Paolo Veronese; the Doge's Palace; and, in the lagoon, the church of S. Spirito in Isola where Titian had painted the three ceiling pieces.

Tintoretto's breathtaking foreshortenings of figures in flight, his silhouettes fringed with radiance, his dramatic bursts of illumination through clouds, the dazzling brushwork, all this Rubens mastered in his twenties. He found the Tintoretto family shop still active, and the material of Jacopo's studio as yet undispersed. From the lightning example of Jacopo, as well as from the more deliberate colour trials and *modelli* of Barocci, he found his own practice of sketching his thoughts directly in oil paint, although he never entirely abandoned the more traditional Renaissance procedure of preparing compositions in chalks or inks (Figs. 1 and 3). His oil sketches, sparkling across the surface of oak panels, seem small works only by the mere computation of inches. Without them the magnitude of his achievement in the Jesuit Church at Antwerp, for example, or in the Medici Cycle (Plate VIII), would have been inconceivable. They were an arena for the surge and play of his invention, as we may see from the marvellous monochrome with his first thoughts for the Whitehall ceiling (Fig. 3). At the stage of realisation in full colour they served in Antwerp as guides to his assistants in painting, or as contract models to show clients. He used oil sketches as handsome alternatives or as supplements to drawings, for instructing precisely engravers whose skill would increase his income, besides advertising and registering his powers of design in an age before international copyright. And he sketched in oils to secure the most satisfactory possible work from silversmiths and from sculptors in marble, from tapestry weavers and from the builders of the *Triumphal Car, celebrating the Victory of Calloo*. His oil sketches were so prized in his lifetime that they were specified for retention in contracts, and even copies of them were listed in the inventories of collectors. His development of this working method, combined with the habit which he had learned from Annibale Carracci in Rome —of revising through life studies drawn in chalks on a bold scale, the postures and gestures of figures before commitment to the final work in painting—was invaluable to every major decorator from Luca Giordano to Tiepolo to Delacroix.

Rubens drew copies of Veronese's gorgeous *Feasts*. And his earliest and tenderest treatment in painting of *The Adoration of the Magi* (Baron Janssen, Uccle), a theme providing abundant opportunities to manage a colourful crowd and display opulent contrasts of flesh and rich stuffs, owes much to Veronese's altarpiece in S. Corona, Vicenza, as well as to an engraving, also of this subject, after Rosso. But his full understanding of the possibilities of Veronese's art for his own came later: in his adaptation of the *Esther before Ahasuerus* in S. Sebastiano for his own ceiling piece of the subject for S. Ignace, Antwerp, and in his reinterpretations of the composition for *The Union of the Two Crowns* on the Whitehall ceiling; in his appreciation of the shimmering play of light in Veronese's drawings, in which taste he made a major repair to one of the drawings in his own collection, Federico Zuccaro's composition for *The Adulteress before Christ*; and triumphantly in this manner of the 1630's, his two versions of the '*Conversation à la Mode*'(Plate XIV), and *The Rape of the Sabines* (Plate XI-XII), where a more vigorous game of love is played between some lusty Flemings, quite convincingly costumed as ancient Romans, and a crowd of women blooming freshly in silks of contemporary fashion.

IN HIS PICTURE OF *The Wise Government of James I* painted for Whitehall, a political allegory based on the iconography of a *Last Judgement*, compositional elements inspired by Tintoretto's *Miracle of St. Mark* and Veronese's *Triumph of Venice* remind us of two persistent loves of Rubens. But the Virtues overcoming the Vices in each of the four elliptical fields at the corners of the Banqueting House Ceiling, dynamic actions envisaged from the outset as part of the programme, show—particularly in *Hercules, as Strength overcoming Envy*—the profit that Rubens had from copying thirty years beforehand Titian's *Cain and Abel* in S. Spirito in Isola. This heroic vein of the late 1530's and 40's had at first attracted Rubens more than the rest of Titian's work: the design of *The Battle of Cadore* to which his own *Battle of the Amazons* (Alte Pinakothek, Munich) was, in part at least, a splendid tribute, engaged him more than the *poesie* painted about 1560 for Philip II. On his first visit to Spain in 1603 he had painted copies of the *Philip II in Armour* and of the head from the *Charles V at Muhlberg*, showing a grasp of outward forms only, without penetration of their inward meaning. This he only attained on his return in 1628-29, during the protracted discussions about the possibilities of peacemaking. Then he was more

experienced; and, apart from some duties as a court portraitist, he had more leisure to approach such masterpieces as *The Rape of Europa* (Prado, Madrid) and *The Fall of Man* (Prado, Madrid). The studies he made then, in front of the Hapsburg Titians, accompanied sometimes by the young Velázquez, were later the foundation of his brilliantly creative reinterpretations of these works, and of those other apparently unsurpassable glories of Titian's art, the Aldobrandini *Bacchanals* from Ferrara, of which he had made some records as a young man in Rome.

AN EXTENSIVE re-education of himself in Madrid and at the Escorial was fortunately possible. But although as a mature and successful artist Rubens could afford to maintain Abraham van Diepenbeeck and others to copy for him in Italy, he was unable after 1608 to return to the masterpieces of sixteenth-century painting and sculpture or to the antiquities of Rome. However, in Rome he had nourished for a lifetime a plastic sense by drawing the Hellenistic and late Roman statues of the Belvedere, and those in the Montalto, Borghese, and Medici collections, thus disciplining his hand and eye. And in Rome, as in Florence, he drew after Michelangelo's works in marble. In his personal renaissance of the antique world he never missed an opportunity to study, and if possible to acquire, coins, cameos, and jewels as well as monumental sculpture. With his pen and brush he exercised his powers to invest comparatively flat or mannered compositions seen in drawings —copies or originals of the Raphael circle—with astonishing relief, semblance of vital movement, and a fresh drama of light and shade. First-hand acquaintance with the work of Raphael himself, produced for the Popes and for Agos-

2. THE PROPHET JEREMIAH, a copy from Michelangelo *Louvre, Paris*

tino Chigi, not only made vivid the foreknowledge which he had gleaned in Antwerp from copies and engravings, but fired him with the ambition to be the impresario of his age; the master of an effective studio organisation producing monumental works of a high standard of execution, whether in painting or in tapestry, and issuing prints to assure the supremacy of his designs.

His understanding of Raphael's *Battle of Constantine*, his own attention to Trajanic reliefs and sarcophagi, the excitement stirred in him by Tintoretto, his decorative sense fascinated by the mannered *contraposti* which Giulio Romano, his predecessor at Mantua, had originated, all contributed to the formation of the sensuous language which triumphs so magniloquently in *The Defeat of Senna-cherib* (Plate IV) and in *The Rape of the Daughters of Leucippus* (Plate VII). These were painted by his own hand throughout, as indeed were both large and small scale works for every year of his career. But with the living example before him of the Carracci organisation in Rome, as well as the works which witnessed the memory of Raphael's, he must have been stimulated early in his career to extend the range of his production by the training of assistants and the use of specialists. The high mark of his genius as an impresario is signified by the way in which assistants of the calibre of Jordaens and Van Dyck could be made to control their idiosyncracies sufficiently to work on different parts of the same picture to Rubens' design—we may think of *The Feast in the House of Simon* (Hermitage, Leningrad) or *Thomyris and the Head of Cyrus* (Museum of Fine Arts, Boston)—without disrupting the unity of the whole Rubensian effect beyond the point which could be controlled by some deft touches of the master's brush.

FOR THOSE WHOSE spirits are too narrow, or stomach too weak, to rejoice in the grand, public performances of Rubens which were commissioned for churches and palaces, he seems more accessible in his more intimate paintings for private devotion (Cover Plate), which sometimes contain idealised portraits of his family, or in the traditionally Flemish specialties: portraiture, landscape and genre. Nothing can be more radiantly happy than his *Self-Portrait with Isabella Brandt in the Honeysuckle Bower* (Plate II), painted in celebration of the auspicious marriage of two healthy, intelligent and well-dressed young people. No wonder that this presentation appealed to Hals, whom Rubens was to meet on his visit to Holland! His happiness was renewed in having, as a widower of fifty-three, married a beautiful girl from his own background, instead of making the expected match to a noblewoman, as he was entitled by his honours from Charles I and Philip IV. His feelings then are beautifully expressed in his *Self-Portrait with Hélèna Fourment and his Son Nicholas in their Garden* (Plate V-VI). This, by a singularly charming invention, is, without affectation, portraiture, landscape and genre in one. The tulips, like the orange trees, shine with the wealth of Rubens, very differently from the flowers which symbolise the transience of human life in *Justus Lipsius and his Pupils*. The loggia and fountain are Italianate, but the old servant who feeds the peacock family was painted from a life study self-consciously drawn in the manner of Pieter Bruegel, a token of Rubens' regard for the greatest Flemish master of the preceding century. And the landscape of *The Return from the Fields* (Plate XV), with its high view point and underlying sense of the coherent structure and movement of terrain, not to speak of the farm people themselves in the foreground, celebrates Bruegel's *August* as well as the country-side near Rubens' house. This landscape of calm observation, although not of literal fact, stands in refreshing contrast to the phrenetic energy of a scene full of such mannerist contortions of form and agitations of lighting as the *Landscape with Philemon and Baucis* (Plate IX).

The Return from the Fields and other landscapes evoking the country round Malines and Elewyt were among those paintings that Rubens retained for his own pleasure. They were in his inventory when he died, together with works by Bruegel, Elsheimer, Brouwer, Van Dyck and many other Flemish and Italian masters. In the course of an exceptionally busy career of painting and diplomacy, he found time to make choice collections also of drawings and antiquities. He published the 'Palazzi di Genova' (1622) besides his share of the 'Electorum Libri II'. With his fellow enthusiasts, Peiresc and Rockox, he planned a book on antique cameos, for which he prepared a number of plates. He had ready for publication a didactic essay 'On the Imitation of Antique Statues', and probably another manuscript 'On Colours'. He remains unchallenged as the most productive of any great European painter. He was blessed with good health as well as a remarkable intelligence. Except for a dangerous attack of pleurisy in Rome, and for the gout which killed him, he had no recorded illnesses; and the only other break in his activity was one holiday of ten days in Portugal with John of Braganza. So it is no wonder that the *Self-Portrait* (Plate XVI), painted in about his sixtieth year, shows a man of distinguished bearing, but a little weary of the world.

3. THE APOTHEOSIS OF JAMES I
By permission of Mrs. Brand, Glynde Place, Sussex

I. THE ANNUNCIATION (*c.* 1609–10)
  Oil on canvas. 88 in. x 78¾ in.
  Kunsthistorisches Museum, Vienna

Rubens painted this *Annunciation* for the Antwerp Sodality of
Married Men. The first of many commissions for the Jesuits, it
was also one of the first works done after his return from Italy.
The influence of Italian painting shows in the steely clarity of
outline, the symmetry of composition and the dramatic contrasts
of lights and darks in the popular style of his contemporary,
Caravaggio. Details such as the carving of the prie-dieu at which
Mary kneels, the lamp and the couch in the background reveal
Rubens' interest in classical design, a fascination which, stimulated by his Italian sojourn, lasted throughout his life as painter
and collector of antiquities.

Even in this early work signs of Rubens' characteristic energy
are present. The whole painting, elaborately composed and
finished as it is, is charged with movement. The angel's cloak,
like a great flame by comparison with the icy blue and white of
the Virgin's garb, billows behind him. At his urgent approach,
Mary starts up and back in surprise. The Holy Spirit descends in
rays of heavenly light, and cherubs hover overhead. In the rush
of wings the lamp gutters and the pages of the prayer book flut-
ter.

II. SELF-PORTRAIT WITH ISABELLA BRANDT IN THE HONEYSUCKLE BOWER (1609–10)
Oil on canvas. 68½ in. x 52 in.
Alte Pinakothek, Munich

Rubens and his first wife were married in 1609. Their union is symbolized in this wedding portrait by the delicate joining of their right hands. The central motif of the painting, it is also central compositionally—and further emphasized by Rubens' left forefinger pointing to it, as well as by the parallel manner in which Isabella's skirt covers his right foot. It cannot be accidental, either, that two sprays of honeysuckle, picked out in the light, hang just above them.

Harmonies of colour and line also express the couple's decorous joy. The restrained tones of their elegant costumes are similar, and Rubens' left leg rhythmically parallels the slight arc of his wife's left arm. Although she sits at his feet—allowing a full view of the splendour of her skirt—she is, because of her high crowned hat, not diminished in stature. And Rubens has further adjusted the difference in height by cropping his own hat just above the brim. Studied arrangement and precise rendition of forms in the Netherlandish tradition are at the heart of this painting which, though a self-portrait of the artist, pretends to be a dual portrait painted by another hand.

III. JUSTUS LIPSIUS AND HIS PUPILS (*c.* 1611–16)
Oil on panel. 66⁴/₅ in. x 57¹/₅ in.
Palazzo Pitti, Florence

Sometimes called *The Four Philosophers*, this is a portrait of the Flemish humanist Justus Lipsius and two of his most brilliant pupils, Rubens' elder brother Philip and Jan van den Wouwere. The painter himself stands in the background behind his brother, his bent arm, seen in perspective, indicating spatial depth. Light falls on the niche with its bust of the Roman philosopher Seneca, and the vase of tulips symbolizing the ever-renewing quality of ancient wisdom. (Lipsius had prepared an edition of Seneca.) In the distant background is a dream-like prospect of Rome, spiritual home of these scholars.

In contrast to their clearly defined figures, Rubens' own form is indistinct; not a participant in their discussion, he looks out towards the observer. In actuality, at the time this painting was done both Lipsius and Philip Rubens were dead. The work has been dated to a few years after Rubens' return from Italy, on the basis of such stylistic evidence as the way the fur and the nap of the table covering have been handled. This tribute to their memory is, then, a composite of earlier portraits, which explains a certain stiffness and lack of interaction among them.

IV. THE DEFEAT OF SENNACHERIB (1613–14)
Oil on panel. 38 in. x 48²/₅ in.
Alte Pinakothek, Munich

The Old Testament story on which this painting is based describes the defeat of the Assyrians led by Sennacherib against Jerusalem. Rubens' interpretation is the essence of Baroque painting with its dramatic lighting, turbulent action and strong, controlling circular and diagonal rhythms.

Thus, the composition can be resolved into a series of concentric circles that give order to the tumult. At the centre is a tightly massed group of rearing horses and dismounted riders, dominated by the turbaned figure of Sennacherib. The terror and confusion of his forces is embodied in the contrast between his falling body and the upward curving thrust of his plunging steed. This motif was a favourite of Rubens, whose draftsmanship and command of form were impressively displayed in paintings of foreshortened, superbly modelled animal bodies. Radiating out from the central unit are the fleeing Assyrians, some illumined by the heavenly radiance, others literally dissolved in darkness. Above is the smaller circle of the avenging angels, their billowing robes repeating the shapes of the clouds. Within these circles all of the forms—limbs and bodies, weapons and battle standards—are seen on the diagonal, building the sensation of pervasive, furious activity.

V-VI. SELF-PORTRAIT WITH HÉLÈNA FOURMENT AND HIS SON NICHOLAS IN THEIR GARDEN (1631)
Oil on panel. 38$^4/_5$ in. x 52$^2/_5$ in.
Alte Pinakothek, Munich

In the year after his second marriage Rubens painted the domestic setting that provided his greatest happiness. His lovely young bride here wears a festive costume *en bergère* (in the style of a shepherdess) and a straw hat trimmed with flowers, perhaps a reference to the goddess Flora. She turns aside to talk with Rubens' son. Arm in arm with his wife, Rubens points with his other hand to a prized possession, symbol of tastes which his wealth and status could now indulge. The Baroque pavilion towards which they stroll is embellished with statuary based on the antique. Somewhat insubstantial in form, it contrasts with the firmly detailed trees and flowers, the dog and exotic fowl. And next to this classical fantasy Rubens has posed the very solid figure of a Flemish peasant.

Unusual for the late Rubens, there is a static quality here. No breeze seems to blow through the foliage in these formal plantings. Only the dog, bounding over to the birds, provides a touch of activity. Not unlike the placid, contained self-portrait with his first wife, this one also makes the pretense of having been posed jointly for another painter.

VII. THE RAPE OF THE DAUGHTERS OF LEUCIPPUS (*c.* 1618)
Oil on canvas. 87⅜ in. x 82¼ in.
Alte Pinakothek, Munich

Hilaira and Phoebe, daughters of King Leucippus, were abducted by twin demigods, Castor and Pollux. Rubens' interpretation of this classical myth has no exact precedent in art. The painter has given his almost sculptural grouping an outdoor setting, and in the clear light the nacreous skin of the young women is set off against the dark skin of their captors. In Baroque fashion the work is built compositionally and psychologically on a series of contrasts.

The rotating pinwheel pattern of forms is held in place by the powerful forward thrust of Pollux' left leg. In contrast to the diagonals of the men's bodies are the concavity of Hilaira's body (held between them) and the convex arch of Phoebe's torso as she is lifted from the ground. The horses turn and paw the air in opposite directions, providing a monumental encircling frame for the human figures. To the animals is given the manifestation of terror and violence implicit in the story. In actuality the women do not struggle. The key to this sensual painting is the fair right hand that rests so lightly on Castor's brawny arm; and the presence of the smiling *putti* (winged cherubs) adds a reassuring note.

VIII. THE EDUCATION OF MARIE DE'MEDICI
(1622–25)
Oil on canvas. 157³/₅ in. x 118 in.
Louvre, Paris

In 1622 Rubens was summoned to Paris by the Queen Mother, Marie de'Medici, to devise a series of paintings for her new Palace of Luxembourg. Among the twenty-one huge canvases representing episodes of her life is this allegory of the young princess' cultural development. She is tutored by various divinities: Minerva, the goddess of Wisdom; Mercury, the winged god of Eloquence (his body sharply foreshortened); and Apollo, playing a viola da gamba. At Apollo's feet is a miniature still life symbolizing the arts—perhaps an allusion to the culture of Marie's native Italy, or to her future role as patroness. Tools of painter, sculptor and musician are grouped together with an antique bust and Minerva's shield with its head of Medusa.

This symbolism has been given an appropriate setting, a grotto on Mt. Parnassus with the Castalian spring, sacred to Apollo and the Muses. Light from above forms a rainbow on the cascade and shines down on the Three Graces who watch over Marie's studies. Just as the light radiates from their translucent skin to illumine the other side of the painting, their presentation of the floral wreath links the composition together.

IX. LANDSCAPE WITH PHILEMON AND BAUCIS
(c. 1625)
Oil on panel. 58⁴/₅ in. x 82¼ in.
Kunsthistorisches Museum, Vienna

The aftermath of a cataclysmic storm is represented here. Flood waters cascade over the countryside, trees are rooted up, a dead steer is caught between two branches. Yet overhead the storm clouds give way to a patch of blue, and below a rainbow arches over the stream. In one bright, dry patch are four figures from classical myth, included by Rubens perhaps to justify this land-scape painting. Almost incidental, dwarfed by the panoramic sweep of the scene, are Philemon and his wife Baucis, aged peasants who alone of their neighbours had provided hospitality to Jupiter and Mercury when they visited the earth in disguise. As a reward, the gods, shown here in characteristic garb, spared the couple's home from the deluge with which they destroyed the land.

At the end of his career Rubens felt no need for classical allu-sions in the sunny, peaceful vistas of Flemish farmland that suc-ceeded such representations of nature in flux. Here, the play of light over an almost fantastically detailed countryside, and the violently contorted forms of tree trunks and foliage, express the characteristic force and energy of the younger Rubens.

X. HÉLÈNA FOURMENT DANDLING HER SON
FRANS (*c.* 1634)
Oil on panel. 66 in. x 46²/₅ in.
Alte Pinakothek, Munich

In 1630 Rubens remarried, and the happiness of life with his
beautiful young bride inspired a new vitality and radiance in his
painting. Hélèna Fourment's face was portrayed often; besides
actual portraits of her alone and with her children, there are
many compositions, secular and religious, in which she was obviously the model for one of the figures. Allowing for differences in
costume and setting, the Cologne *Holy Family* (Cover), for
example, recalls this mother-and-child group.

In this painting Hélèna is seen, a young woman of fashion, with
her first-born son Frans. Despite the elegant clothes and the
hints of classical architecture and elaborately carved furniture,
there is an unposed informality to this oil sketch. The painter-
father has obviously been amused and delighted by posing the
child in a dashing velvet cap. Warmth and intimacy are transmit-
ted by the quick, loose brushwork. Rubens' sure touch manages,
without elaborate finishing, to give the feeling of the different
textures of his wife's gown, especially the material gauzy enough
to reveal some of the pattern and colour of the skirt under it. And
he delicately contrasts the skin tones, creamy where the light
hits, rosy where faintly shadowed.

XI-XII. THE RAPE OF THE SABINES (*c.* 1635)
Oil on panel. 66¾ in. x 92 in.
National Gallery, London

Romulus, founder of Rome, in an effort to provide wives for the settlers of the province, invited the neighbouring Sabines to a festival. At his signal the Romans fell upon the Sabine women and carried them off. Rubens, like Poussin in the next century and Picasso in ours, made use of this legendary historical episode and by purposeful anachronisms suggested its contemporary relevance. His ancient warriors and their victims wear seventeenth-century Flemish garb; the architecture is that of imperial Rome.

Perhaps because of the bravura painting and the loveliness of the women—Hélèna Fourment may have been the model for the matron in the centre foreground—some critics feel that the work is festive in tone. But the ugly violence of the story is only slightly softened by dramatic composition and lighting, and by rhythmic movement. Force, resistance and lamentation are the essential themes, conveyed by the overall diagonal sweeping from upper left to lower right and repeated insistently throughout the work by other diagonals: arms that implore and arms that reach out to capture, bodies that struggle away and others that move to overpower this struggle.

XIII. PORTRAIT OF SUSANNE FOURMENT (*c.* 1625)
Oil on panel. 31 in. x 21½ in.
National Gallery, London

This portrait owes its popularity to the sunny radiance that began to characterize Rubens' later work. In the clear outdoor light the creamy flesh tones, imperceptibly shadowed by the hat brim, seem almost transparent. The large dark eyes and the crystal eardrops catch and play with this light in their different ways. Contrasts of light and shadow model the folds of the sleeves, their crispness contrasted with the gauziness of shawl and blouse. The demure, contained pose is animated by colour: the glowing red in the sleeves, the soft blue of the sky. Line, too, enlivens. The rhythmic diagonal sweep of the hat brim is countered and echoed by the little swirling movements of the feathers. Feathers, fleecy clouds, the bows on her shoulder all contribute to the vibrancy.

With some dissent, it is generally thought that the sitter was Hélèna Fourment's older sister Susanne, whose portrait Rubens did several times. All scholars agree that the name by which the painting has long been known, *Le Chapeau de Paille,* is obviously an error. The hat is felt, not straw, and 'paille' has been substituted for a similar word meaning the ceremonial canopy used to shelter notable personages.

XIV. 'CONVERSATION À LA MODE' (*c.* 1635) — *Detail*
Oil on canvas. 79$^{1}/_{5}$ in. x 113$^{1}/_{5}$ in.
Prado, Madrid

This is part of a very large painting showing elegantly dressed couples, attended by cupids, at an outdoor festival in honour of Venus. (The work is sometimes known as *The Garden of Love*.) Under a fountain, at the extreme right of the picture, the cavalier and his lady step down to join the other lovers who disport themselves flirting and chatting. A depiction of Flemish upper class social diversion, the work may actually portray some of Rubens' circle. Although the subject later became popular with French painters, notably Watteau, their treatment lacks the allegorical element found here. Symbols of wedlock and conjugal love are scattered throughout the painting.

Beyond its painterly quality, this detail is an effective composition in its own right. The left arms, bent at the same angle, make a diagonal leading the couple into the composition. This compelling line is repeated above in the sweep of the man's broad hat, lightly echoed in the curve of the woman's ostrich fan. The free and unlaboured brushwork gives the illusion of silk so lustrous it reflects the red of the man's costume. Against the woman's neck her earring dangles with *trompe l'oeil* effect.

XV. THE RETURN FROM THE FIELDS
(1635–38) — *Detail*
Oil on panel. 48^4/$_5$ in. x 78 in.
Palazzo Pitti, Florence

Late in life Rubens turned from formal, commissioned work to pictures of his family and to landscapes for his own pleasure. This is a view out over the fields near his country residence, the Château de Steen. The scene unfolds in a series of details which Rubens makes sure the observer lingers over. The eye is slowly drawn along by the curving file of sheep or by the diagonal line of the brook into the middle distance, and then along a line of trees running diagonally in the opposite direction up to the top centre. The horizon is not a strong line of demarcation: the vista goes on as if reluctant to fade out.

Quite different from earlier landscapes, settings for classical myths in which an agitated, dramatic presentation of nature prevails (as in Plate IX), this is a domestic picture, celebrating the joys of harvest and the tranquil beauty of the flat fields. The peasants here are not dwarfed by their surroundings but are an essential part of the scene. Soft golden light and air are its components, peace and fulfillment its message.

XVI. SELF-PORTRAIT (1638–40)
Oil on canvas. 43³/₅ in. x 33¹/₅ in.
Kunsthistorisches Museum, Vienna

Rubens' last self-portrait, painted shortly before his death, shows clearly the traces of age and illness in the heavy eyes and sagging lines of the face. Nevertheless, there is dash and distinction in his bearing. Rubens was still working actively, his painting and drawing ever more spontaneous and assured—as evidenced here. Dramatically effective lighting reveals the somewhat disillusioned face, the fine ruffle that relieves the sombre tone of his costume, and his hands. One rests on his sword, symbol of his diplomatic career; the other, his painting hand, is gloved either in reference to the crippling gout (or arthritis) that afflicted him, or in reminiscence of a famous painting well known to him, Titian's *Man with a Glove*.

In the dim glow, the base of a column is seen, its carving alluding to Rubens' passion for classical design. Beyond this there are no details of setting, and the composition is fittingly one of restraint and dignity. Interestingly, in none of his self-portraits did the painter ever depict himself as such. He is always the courtier or family man; elegantly costumed, he may hold a sword but never the tools of his art.